INDOOR PLANT SELECTION AND SURVIVAL GUIDE

by Terrestris

Grosset & Dunlap
Publishers
New York

Published in association with *Parade Magazine*

Sansevieria (snake plant), 2'

The plant on the title page is a 2½' *Dracaena warneckei*.
Size range for this and other plants is given in the Indoor
Plant Selection and Survival Chart on pp. 26-27.

CONTENTS

TERRESTRIS AND ITS GUIDE

Terrestris (the Latin word for terrestrial, meaning "of the earth") is one of the nation's largest suppliers of indoor plants, and one of the few with their own nurseries, trucking facilities, and retail outlets. The nurseries are located in Puerto Rico and Florida, and the main retail outlet is in the heart of the largest market in the country, the New York Metropolitan Area. In Manhattan, the center of this area, Terrestris has covered a large rooftop with spectacular greenhouses. In this botanical atmosphere they maintain a tremendous display with thousands of indoor plants ranging in size from six inches to eighteen feet. Over the years, Terrestris has sold hundreds of thousands of indoor plants and installed and maintained numerous residential and commercial plantings. This practical experience has given Terrestris the knowledge which plants will survive best and how to care for them. This is the knowledge on which this book is based.

Terrestris is convinced that anyone can have success with indoor plants. They know that many people may doubt this, especially if they've failed with plants—or even given up before trying after hearing of friends' bad experiences. But Terrestris has found that, in almost every case, the consumer is simply unaware of a few facts that could guarantee his success.

Though indoor plants have always been popular in Europe, they have only recently become widely popular in the United States. With the growing interest in ecology and the natural environment, people are becoming more aware of the satisfaction a living, growing plant can give to indoor surroundings. This great interest makes it important that consumers know how to properly select and

Dizygotheca, 3'

care for their plants. The many books on the subject are generally written for the hobbyist, are too long, and are not sufficiently specific. Terrestris' commercial experience has taught them that most people buying plants only want to know which plants will survive best and how to care for them properly with the least effort.

To fill this need, Terrestris prepared a sixteen-page plant selection and care guide for their greenhouse customers. During the past year, over 100,000 copies have been distributed. Terrestris has now expanded the guide into this concise handbook. It describes how to choose the right plant for your conditions—the first but by far the most important step when buying a plant—and gives care instructions which are easy to learn and follow. This handbook will help you select those plants which will survive and flourish in your environment.

TWO-MINUTE GUIDE TO BUYING A PLANT

Environmental Factors to Consider

Light Before buying your plant, the factor you must consider first is whether you have enough light for the plant you choose. Read *Measuring Your Light* on pp. 14–17 to determine how much light you have. Then look at the Survival Chart in the center of this book to learn which plants can live in your light. A key on the chart tells you where they are pictured. Remember, plants do well with more light than their rating suggests but cannot be healthy in less light. See *Light*, p. 12.

Hardiness A plant with a rating of excellent will survive best. The Survival Chart rates the hardiness of each plant. See *Hardiness*, p. 12.

Tall Plants Don't get your plant too tall. The top of the plant should be below the top of your window unless you are using artificial light. See *Using Large Plants*, p. 8.

Watering Don't be concerned about this. Whatever is required you can read about and control after you get your plant. See *Watering*, p. 32.

Temperature and Humidity Don't be concerned about this either. The temperature and humidity that people live in are fine for any of the plants we list. See *Temperature* and *Humidity*, p. 31.

Aglaonema (Chinese evergreen), 15″–2′

Consumer Protections to Consider

You want to be sure the plant is healthy before you buy it and is not overpriced. See *Consumer Protections,* p. 23.

Care Factors to Consider

Fertilizer All plants, even the smallest, must be continually fertilized for good health. Be sure to get fertilizer when you select your plant. See *Fertilizer,* p. 35.

Insect and Fungus Control Insects are everywhere. There is very little chance your plants will remain free of insects and fungus unless you periodically spray them preventively with insecticide and fungicide. See *Insect and Fungus Control,* p. 40.

Drainage Water The container your plant is grown in has drainage holes in the bottom. Be sure you have a saucer or decorative container in which to catch the drainage water.

Other Care Items There are a few other care items in addition to those mentioned here. You don't need to be concerned with them until after you get your plant. They are all covered in this book.

Aphelandra (zebra plant), 1′

HOW TO SELECT YOUR PLANT

This section describes everything you need to know before buying your plant, including light, which is also a crucial care factor.

Using Large Plants

Don't hesitate to invest in large plants. They are as easy to take care of as small ones, and a large plant will enhance any indoor environment far more than is generally realized. Using big plants is one of the most satisfying and practical ways to achieve decorative and dramatic effects for small cost.

Be sure to measure your ceiling height before selecting your large plants. If you are relying on natural light from a window, measure from the floor to the top of the window. The top of the plant should be a foot below the top of the window unless the plant is right against the window. And be sure to take actual measurements of the plants you select, as sizes in a greenhouse or store can be deceiving.

8

Areca, 6'

Rate of Plant Growth

Although plants grow fairly rapidly in the tropics, they generally grow slowly indoors. Decreased light, humidity, and temperatures account for this reduced rate of growth. The fastest-growing large plants will seldom exceed a foot of growth a year even with more than the recommended minimum of light.

Ficus elastica (rubber plant), 2′, 7′

Schefflera (umbrella plant), 4', 9'

Hardiness

As you'll see from the Survival Chart in the center of this book, Terrestris rates plants in three degrees of hardiness—excellent, good and fair. This hardiness refers to the ability of plants to grow and remain healthy under indoor conditions. The plant is as hardy as rated only when it has at least the minimum light recommended, and when it is watered and otherwise cared for as outlined in this care guide. Therefore, a Ficus exotica which is rated as requiring good light and has a hardiness rating of excellent would not be hardy if it had anything less than good light.

There are literally tens of thousands of tropical plants. Of these, only about one thousand have any chance of surviving indoors. Of these thousand, less than a hundred have proven to be suitable for most indoor environments. And of these hundred, we rate only nineteen as excellent in hardiness. These are the plants with which most people will have the most success.

We have also included plants with ratings of good and fair, but none which we would rate poor in hardiness.

Light

Light is the least considered, yet the most important single factor in maintaining indoor plants successfully. A plant must have light in order to convert the elements it obtains from soil and fertilizer into energy, which it uses to produce new plant growth.

Amazingly, some plants can live with insufficient light and look well for many months, drawing on their stored food. This healthy appearance is deceiving, because in reality the plant is seriously weakening. Even though it may later be put into sufficient light, it will probably never regain full health. Be careful when you buy a plant. Regardless of how healthy it looks, be sure it has not been kept in insufficient light for too long.

Philodendron selloum (fingerleaf), 3′

The amount of light a plant needs is more than most people realize. Too often we are misled by seeing healthy-looking plants in locations where there is actually insufficient light. Airports, lobbies, offices, department stores, shopping malls, etc. often have plants which don't get enough light. It never shows because as a rule they are replaced repeatedly with new ones under contracts with greenhouses. Many magazines and advertisements use plants as decorative items. These plants will often be placed where they look best, even though there may be insufficient light in that location. Don't be confused by healthy-looking plants in locations with less light than Terrestris recommends.

This guide only concerns plants which don't flower indoors but whose decorative beauty comes from their foliage alone. Foliage plants survive on very little light compared to what they would get outdoors but by indoor standards they require a considerable amount. For example, a well-lit office will seldom have more than Low Light at desk level. A measurement taken only 10 feet back but still directly in front of an unobstructed south window provides only Low Light. This illustrates that the minimum rating of Good Light that certain indoor plants require is bright by indoor standards.

Cissus rhombifolia (grape ivy), 1½'

Light Ratings

Terrestris' light ratings of Low, Medium, or Good which are given for each plant indicate the minimum amount of light needed for healthy growth. Almost all plants will grow better with more than the recommended minimum light. Plants sometimes live in lower light levels than those recommended but usually will have reduced growth, shorter life, and a strong chance of poor health. If there is not sufficient natural light, artificial light (see p. 18) may be used as a supplement. Artificial light may also be the only light source in the absence of natural light.

In order to rate your available light, it will be necessary for you to take a light measurement. This measurement can be taken either with or without a light meter, as the next few pages will explain.

Measuring Your Light without a Light Meter

If at all possible, measure your light with a photographic light meter as described at the end of this section. Otherwise, you can use the written descriptions given below as a guide in measuring your light.
on the next page as a guide in measuring your light.

14

These ratings are based on light from a 3′x5′ window. If the window is not that size, make allowances. An obstructed window as used below is one from which about half the sky is blocked by trees, buildings, curtains, or other obstructions as seen from where the plant will be placed. The ratings are also based on the top of the plant being at least a foot below the top of the window. Distances are taken from the center of the plant.

LOW LIGHT

4′ back from an obstructed North window
6′ back from or at the edge of an unobstructed North window
6′ back from or at the edge of an obstructed East or West window
8′ back from or 1′ to the side of an unobstructed East or West window
8′ back from or 1′ to the side of an obstructed South window
10′ back from or 2′ to the side of an unobstructed South window

MEDIUM LIGHT

4′ back from an unobstructed North window
4′ back from an obstructed East or West window
5′ back from or at the edge of an unobstructed East or West window
6′ back from or at the edge of an obstructed South window
8′ back from or 1′ to the side of an unobstructed South window

GOOD LIGHT

2′ back from an obstructed East or West window
3′ back from an unobstructed East or West window
4′ back from an obstructed South window
5′ back from or at the edge of an unobstructed South window

Measuring Your Light with a Light Meter

The most accurate way to measure your light is with a photographic light meter. This is very easy to do when you follow these simple instructions. Remember, many cameras have built-in light meters. Take your measurements when the sun is at its highest point.

• Set the ASA film speed index on the light meter or camera to 200. Next, set the dial on your light meter or camera lens to 1/125 of a second shutter speed.

• Use a piece of white paper about 24″ square. Place the paper where the top third of the foliage of the plant will be located and face the flat surface of the paper toward your maximum light source.

Tradescantia (wandering Jew), 2′

Pothos, 2′

Chamaedorea elegans (Neanthe bella), 2½′

• Aim your light meter or camera with built-in light meter at the paper. Get close enough to the paper so the meter sees only the white paper. Be sure that you don't block the light source and cast a shadow on the paper.

• If you were taking a picture of that piece of white paper, the light meter would tell you at what f stop (lens opening) to set your camera. By using the table below, this f stop will tell you how much light you have.

f 5.6	=	Low Light
f 8	=	Medium Light
f 11	=	Good Light

It makes no difference in your measurements whether your light source is natural or artificial or a combination of both. If you see that the light level is decreasing as a season changes, be sure and check the light again to make sure it has not dropped below the minimum.

Phoenix (date palm), 3′

Using Artificial Light

When natural light is lacking or insufficient, artificial light may be used. It can be either a supplement or the only light source. The various factors you should consider when using artificial light are given below. A word of caution—light bulbs and fluorescent tubes emit as little as *half* their light towards the end of their life. Unless you recheck your light reading it is best to replace bulbs or tubes about halfway through their rated life. All artificial light information is from the most recent experimentation conducted by the United States Department of Agriculture at Beltsville, Maryland.

Succulents, 1′

Fluorescent Tubes These are excellent sources of light for plants. Contrary to common belief, special tubes designed for growing plants are no better than ordinary cool white tubes when considering lighting for foliage plants. Fluorescent tubes consume very little electricity for the amount of light they produce. Their main disadvantage is that they are bulky and decoratively more limited than bulbs.

Mercury Vapor Reflector Bulbs Mercury vapor light is as good as fluorescent for foliage plants. It is an extremely efficient light source, a 175-watt mercury vapor bulb producing the equivalent of almost 400 watts of incandescent lighting. Initially, mercury vapor is more expensive than incandescent, as it must have a vapor bulb and a separate transformer (called ballast) to convert normal current into special starting and running current. It pays for itself, however, in less than a year's time in electrical savings alone, and the bulb itself lasts 12 times as long as an incandescent.

Incandescent Reflector Bulbs While less desirable, incandescent reflector bulbs are still a satisfactory light source for tropical foliage plants. They are initially very inexpensive and are the most decoratively flexible to use. No special type of incandescent light is better than any other as an artificial light source, when lighting foliage plants.

Light Position In order for a plant to maintain its natural shape, it should receive its light from an evenly distributed source, at least above the middle of the plant. It is possible for a plant to receive light only from below, but the light rating must be above the recommended minimum. Even then, the plant will tend to become heavier at the bottom and somewhat change its natural shape. See *Rotating the Plant,* p. 30.

Light Duration If the amount of artificial light equals only the minimum rating recommended for the particular plant, then the light must be on for 16 hours a day, every day. If the light is almost double the minimum amount, then this duration can be reduced to 12 hours.

If used to supplement natural light, artificial lighting should be on only during daylight hours, as a plant should have a dark period. It is, however, better to have light 24 hours a day than to have too little light.

Light Concentration Light from a bulb spreads out rapidly unless a reflector is used to concentrate the light into one area. Generally, when lighting a plant, all the light should be concentrated on the plant. The farther away a bulb is, the narrower the beam of light needs to be in order to keep the light focused on the plant. If the bulb must be fairly far away, a spotlight may be necessary to concentrate the light beam on the plant.

Heat Heat generated by an artificial light source must be carefully watched. If the temperature on the surface of the leaves goes above 85°F. the light is too close and the leaf will no longer carry out photosynthesis (the necessary conversion through light of food to energy which sustains the plant and produces new growth). Even in the tropics, where the sun is the sole light source, plants can only do this during those hours when leaf temperatures are below 85°F. But the sun is never concentrated full strength at all times on a plant as an arti-

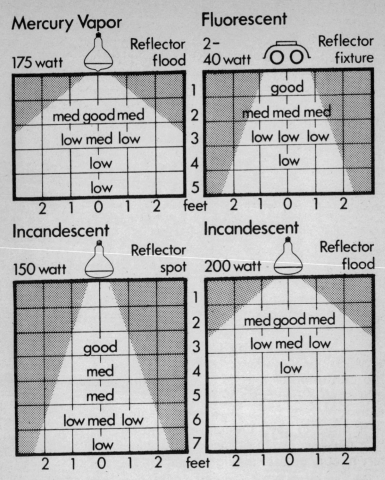

Mercury Vapor
175 watt — Reflector flood

	1
med good med	2
low med low	3
low	4
low	5

2 1 0 1 2 feet

Fluorescent
2- 40 watt — Reflector fixture

good	1
med med med	2
low low low	3
low	4

2 1 0 1 2

Incandescent
150 watt — Reflector spot

	1
	2
good	3
med	4
med	5
low med low	6
low	7

2 1 0 1 2 feet

Incandescent
200 watt — Reflector flood

	1
med good med	2
low med low	3
low	4

2 1 0 1 2

These charts show the amount of light produced by various artificial light sources at the distances given. The ratings of good, medium, and low light are equivalent to those given for natural light on p. 15. These charts can also serve as a guide for other size bulbs not shown.

ficial light would be. So if the leaf surfaces feel warm to the touch, chances are the leaf temperature is above 85°F. and the light should be moved farther away from the plant.

Dracaena marginata, 4', 7'

Consumer Protections

If you follow this guide, you will have solved the main problem in buying a plant. This is knowing which plant will survive in the amount of light available where you plan to put the plant. With the guide, you'll know more about how much light plants require indoors than many people who sell plants.

While not as important, there are a few other factors which should be considered when buying a plant. There is little quality control by the government or growers associations, particularly with regard to the proper rooting of plants. Many plants, even large plants, are rooted from cuttings. A 12' Ficus exotica tree (see p. 39) actually can be a branch cut from a much larger tree which has been subsequently rooted in a pot. Dracaena massangeana (see p. 38) is almost always grown using stalks of larger plants which are put into pots; there they root and then sprout new foliage at the top of the stalks. In this way a number of shorter plants are grown from a single tall plant. The problem you must watch for is that although such plants will often have beautiful foliage, they will not have grown a good root structure.

How can you tell? Roots coming out the drainage holes indicate that the plant has at least some roots, but often the very first roots find their way out these holes. The best way to check proper rooting is to tap the plant out of its pot. If a few roots can be seen around the bottom and, even better, around the sides of the pot, you can be assured of proper rooting. This is not always practical, so you can resort to another test. Tug gently at a stem or stalk. A little play sideways and even upwards is not a bad sign. But if it seems that with very little pull you would be able to lift the stem or stalk right out of the pot, pass up that plant—no matter how beautiful the foliage looks.

Another important matter to consider is whether your plant has been light-starved when you buy it. This subject is covered in the second paragraph under *Light,* p. 12.

Insects and fungus can be a problem if the infestation is bad enough to have weakened the plant. If the plant you've selected is the only one of its type you can conveniently choose, a minor insect problem is not that serious, provided you are aware of it and treat the plant as soon as you get it. While fungus can also be eliminated, it is more difficult to control, and the extent to which it may have damaged the plant can be less easily observed. How to identify the presence of soil and foliage insects is covered under *Insect and Fungus Control,* pp. 40–42.

It is very seldom that a plant for sale will have a disease, but if it does there is rarely any cure. If a plant looks weak or unhealthy and if you cannot identify the problem, don't take a chance.

We cannot stress too strongly that the most important consideration is light. If the plant you buy seems to be healthy and if you are sure through following this guide that it is the proper plant for the amount you have, you will have little chance of trouble.

About Prices

Prices of most things are increasing, but when an industry experiences rapid growth, prices can often drop. The indoor plant industry has undergone such an expansion and prices of indoor plants have decreased accordingly in most cases, certainly in ours.

This means comparison shopping is worthwhile for the consumer, since prices can vary not only from store to store, but from plant to plant within a store. In selecting yours, you should compare carefully, as no two plants are alike. Measure height, consider fullness, and be sure you are comparing the same variety of plant.

Chamaedorea seifritzii (bamboo palm), 6′

Indoor Plant Selection and Survival Chart

Page if illus-trated	PROPER NAME	Hardiness see page 12	Watering see page 32	Smallest size generally available	Largest size generally available	Largest size occasion-ally available

Low Light or better (page 15)

Page if illus-trated	PROPER NAME	Hardiness	Watering	Smallest	Largest	Largest occasional
7	Aglaonema	Excel	Med	15"	2'	
	Aspidistra	Excel	Med	2'	3'	
17	Chamaedorea elegans	Excel	Med	18"	3'	
	Dracaena godseffiana	Good	Mod	6"	1'	
22	Dracaena marginata	Excel	Mod	1'	8'	12'
38	Dracaena massangeana	Excel	Mod	2'	8'	12'
36	Dracaena sandriana	Good	Mod	6"	15"	
56	Dracaena warneckei	Excel	Mod	1'	3'	4'
63	Filices (ferns)	Fair	Hvy	1'	2'	6'
52	Kentia	Excel	Hvy	4'	6'	7'
63	Nephthytis	Excel	Med	6"	15"	
36	Philodendron cordatum	Excel	Mod	6"	9"	
50	Philodendron pertusum	Excel	Mod	2'	4'	6'
13	Philodendron selloum	Excel	Mod	18"	4'	6'
	Philodendron (other)	Excel	Mod			
2	Sansevieria	Excel	Mod	6"	3'	
43	Spathiphyllum	Excel	Hvy	15"	4'	

Medium Light or better (page 15)

Page if illus-trated	PROPER NAME	Hardiness	Watering	Smallest	Largest	Largest occasional
	Ardisia	Good	Med	9"	2'	
45	Asparagus	Fair	Med	9"	18"	
	Aucuba	Fair	Mod	9"	2'	
	Caladium	Fair	Hvy	1'	2'	
44	Chamaedorea erumpens	Excel	Med	3'	7'	12'
25	Chamaedorea seifritzii	Excel	Med	3'	7'	12'
	Chamaerops humilis	Fair	Med	18"	5'	
43	Chlorophytum	Good	Med	9"	18"	
	Cissus antarctica	Good	Med	9"	18"	
14	Cissus rhombifolia	Good	Med	9"	18"	
	Coleus	Fair	Hvy	6"	18"	
	Cordyline	Fair	Med	9"	6'	
35	Dieffenbachia	Good	Med	15"	3'	
	Fatsia	Good	Med	18"	2'	
10	Ficus elastica	Excel	Mod	18"	7'	10'
	Fittonia	Good	Med	9"	1'	
	Maranta	Fair	Med	6"	18"	
37	Peperomia	Good	Mod	6"	1'	
	Pilea	Good	Med	9"	1'	
46	Pleomele	Good	Mod	18"	6'	8'
16	Pothos	Good	Mod	9"	1'	
	Rhapis	Fair	Med	4'	6'	
11	Schefflera	Excel	Mod	2'	8'	18'
45	Tolmiea	Fair	Hvy	9"	15"	
16	Tradescantia	Good	Med	9"	18"	

26

Indoor Plant Selection and Survival Chart

Page if illustrated	PROPER NAME	Hardiness see page 12	Watering see page 32	Smallest size generally available	Largest size generally available	Largest size occasionally available
	Good Light or better (page 15)					
	Agave	Good	Mod	1'	2'	
8	Aphelandra	Fair	Hvy	9"	1'	
41	Araucaria	Good	Med	1'	6'	10'
9	Areca	Fair	Hvy	3'	6'	12'
61	Beaucarnea	Good	Mod	1'	4'	6'
31	Cactus[1]	Good	[1]	6"	6'	
49	Crassula	Good	Mod	9"	1'	3'
	Croton	Fair	Mod	18"	4'	
	Cycas	Fair	Mod	2'	4'	6'
5	Dizygotheca	Good	Mod	9"	7'	12'
62	Euphorbia	Good	Mod	9"	3'	4'
39	Ficus exotica[2]	Excel	Mod	30"	12'	18'
47	Ficus lyrata	Fair	Mod	2'	6'	7'
	Gynura	Fair	Med	6"	8"	
	Hedera	Good	Med	6"	9"	
	Helxine	Fair	Med	4"	5"	
61	Hoya	Good	Mod	5"	6"	
18	Phoenix	Good	Med	15"	6'	8'
30	Pittosporum	Fair	Mod	9"	3'	
	Plectranthus	Good	Med	9'	18"	
55	Podocarpus	Fair	Med	6"	5'	15'
34	Polyscias	Excel	Mod	9"	8'	10'
19	Succulents	Good	Mod	6"	1'	
28	Yucca	Good	Mod	4'	8'	12'

[1]See special cactus watering instructions on p. 33.

[2]*Ficus exotica* is usually considered the most attractive of the small-leaved *Ficus*, particularly after the leaves have thinned out under indoor conditions. *Ficus benjamina, retusa,* and *philippinense* are also small-leaved and generally available. They all require the same light and the same care.

About This Chart

The plants in this chart are both generally available and suitable for the indoor environment. Those most suitable and widely available are also shown in pictures. Common names are given in the index. The book covers only foliage plants, so no flowering plants are listed.

Yucca, 5′

HOW TO CARE FOR YOUR PLANT

This section describes everything you need to know in caring for your plant. You should also take into account light and other care factors described in *HOW TO SELECT YOUR PLANT*.

Acclimation

Tropical plants normally shed their old leaves fairly evenly over the course of a year. However, when a plant's environment changes, it will often react by losing a lot of leaves suddenly. This does not necessarily mean a problem. It is one of the plant's ways of protecting itself from a difficult situation. If the plant is moved into less light than it had before, it will lose leaves since it cannot support as much foliage in a lower light level. If the plant is subjected to unusually cool temperatures (not below freezing as this will kill tropical plants), it will lose leaves but it will grow new ones. Plants will also sometimes lose leaves simply when being moved from one location to another but again, they will grow new ones.

When you first get your plant, you should not be concerned if foliage turns yellow and drops off. On a full plant as much as a third of the leaves can be shed. After the initial adjustment period of up to a month, the appearance of yellow leaves will slow down. Then there should be as many new leaves growing as there are old ones turning yellow.

Pittosporum, 2½'

Rotating the Plant

If the light source is from one side only and provides no more than the minimum light rating required, the plant will survive but will thin out on the side away from the light. It is not wise to rotate such a plant, since the side getting the light must get its full daily minimum without interruption for the plant to remain decorative and healthy. If, however, the light is the next rating above the minimum, you can rotate the plant weekly to maintain its even shape. Light from above will maintain the plant's even shape without rotation. See *Light Position,* p. 20.

Temperature

Indoor plants are by necessity tropical plants whose natural environment provides warm temperatures all year. Temperatures normally comfortable for people are satisfactory for most tropical plants which are kept indoors. Be careful where you place your plants. You would not sit comfortably all day in the direct draft of an air conditioner or on top of a hot radiator. Most plants prefer to be 10°-15°F. cooler at night, but this is not overly important. Remember, freezing temperatures will kill tropical plants.

Humidity

Most tropical plants prefer high humidity. However, the tropical plants most commonly used indoors do not require high humidity for good health. Homes and commercial locations, particularly those with hot-air heat and air conditioning, usually have low humidity. This is not a problem, provided the plant is properly cared for, especially with regard to watering.

"Misting" by spraying water on the plant has little use unless it is repeated every few minutes because the water dries up so quickly. Commercially, this is done mainly during propagation with automatic equipment. Putting your plants in trays with water and gravel may be attractive and practical for drainage but the added humidity produced is generally too little to benefit indoor plants.

Cacti, 6"–1'

Watering

A plant should never receive a set amount of water or be on a routine watering schedule. Moisture in the air, the season, temperature, light, whether the pot is porous, and many other factors influence the frequency of watering. We recommend determining how often to water by feeling and observing the soil, not by observing a time schedule.

Whatever plant you have, you must always water it well enough to completely saturate the soil. Some excess water should always come out the bottom of the pot, otherwise sufficient water may never reach the bottom, where most of the roots are located. However, never let a plant sit in excess water for more than a couple of days, as this can rot the roots. With larger containers, a good method is to water two or three times, a few minutes apart. This gives the water a chance to soak slowly through the soil. Too often, water will run down a crack between the soil and the pot and out the drainage holes, without soaking all the way through to all the roots. If the soil has shrunk away from the container, press it back firmly against the side of the container, adding a little soil if necessary. Each plant on our Chart takes one of the three following water levels.

Heavy Watering Plant should be kept constantly moist. Soil should always be damp enough so that moisture easily can be felt when you press your finger in the soil. The soil should not, however, be soggy wet.

Medium Watering Plant should be heavily watered to ensure that the entire pot is thoroughly saturated. After the heavy watering, wait until just the surface soil has become powder dry to the touch before watering again.

Moderate Watering Plant should be heavily watered to ensure the entire pot is thoroughly saturated. After watering, allow the soil to become powder dry: 2" down on pots 17" in diameter and over; 1" down on pots 12" in diameter; ½″ down on pots 8″ in diameter; only on the surface on pots 6″ in diameter and less. While this drying out is important, be sure to water promptly as soon as the soil has dried out to the degree indicated.

Watering Plants Which Are Unhealthy or Have Insufficient Light

It is important to reduce watering when plants are unhealthy for any reason, or in light lower than the minimum recommended. In both cases the frequency of watering should be cut below the recommended normal level. Under these conditions a plant's root system is weak and subject to rot. It must dry out more than usual between waterings. A plant under these conditions in a large container (17″ diameter or over) can go as much as two months between waterings.

Cactus Watering

In the desert, a cactus has roots to collect water the few times it rains. Between rains, it uses this water, which is stored in its body. In a humid greenhouse, the cactus theoretically doesn't need roots nor does it need watering, since it can easily get its required moisture through its skin. In a dry indoor environment (still not as dry as the desert), watering every two months in winter and once a month in summer is sufficient. Cactuses do best in clay pots which help evaporate excess moisture quickly and keep the soil dry.

Terrarium Watering

Terrariums, particularly if they have lids, require very little water. Wait until the surface of the soil becomes dry, then water lightly. Try to avoid having any standing water collect at the bottom. Look carefully through the glass to make sure this doesn't happen. If condensation inside is so heavy that you cannot see in, remove the lid until the inside is visible.

33

Polyscias (Ming tree), 6′

Fertilizer

All plants are fertilized continually during the period they are professionally grown. Indoor plants are in pots where the roots cannot spread out over a large area to reach the necessary nutriments for the plant. Confined to a container, they use all the food value present in the soil within a few months. Once the food value is used, plants will draw on their own stored energy, but once this is gone they must gain strength from water and light alone. Water and light may keep a plant alive, but growth will be slower and the general health and appearance of the plant will be poor. It is therefore very important to give a plant fertilizer (sometimes called plant food or vitamins).

Dieffenbachia (dumbcane), 2½′

35

Philodendron cordatum, 2'   *Dracaena sandriana, 1½'*

While there are many different kinds available, we recommend using a slow-release type. Slow-release fertilizers are treated in such a way that they will automatically release nutriments to the plant over a period of six months to a year, depending on the type used. With the more commonly known water-soluble fertilizers, application is required about every 10 days. As this is extra work and hard to remember, plants usually are more sure of getting needed nutriments when a long-range slow-release fertilizer is used.

The basic elements all plants require are:

nitrogen—for healthy green foliage
phosphorus—for strong roots
potash—for increased resistance,
    particularly to disease

Peperomia, 9″

Plants often also require very small quantities of a few other elements:

manganese	zinc
iron	boron
copper	molybdenum

These are called trace elements. Sometimes they will be included in a basic fertilizer formulation, but to get all of them it is usually necessary to buy a separate trace element fertilizer. This type of fertilizer is also available in slow-release form.

Dracaena massangeana, 3', 6'

Ficus exotica, 4', 7'

Insect and Fungus Control

Insect and fungus control for indoor plants can be quite simple. In this short section Terrestris explains what you should know to protect your plants from these problems.

Foliage Insects

Foliage insects can easily find their way indoors. With few of their normal natural enemies present, they thrive and multiply unless eliminated. The simplest way of ensuring that your plants are not infested with insects is to spray them with a good plant insecticide once a month. Terrestris strongly recommends this preventive procedure. In this way, insects will be eliminated before they can do damage or multiply. If, however, you find that a plant is infested with insects, it should be sprayed every week until they are gone.

We recommend using a spray with some systemic action. Systemic insecticides are those which are absorbed by the plant and make it poisonous to sucking insects for up to a month. Use a concentrated insecticide which you dilute in water and spray on the plant. Do not save any diluted insecticide mixture as it loses its potency shortly after being mixed. Aerosol sprays are unsatisfactory, as too much insecticide is vaporized into the air. Also, the best types of insecticides are not available in aerosol cans.

You should learn to recognize foliage insects and their damage. The most common indoor plant insects are spider mites, mealy bugs, and scale.

Spider mites are the most common and the most harmful. They leave a dirty, dusty weblike deposit. They soon make the leaves they are sucking mottled, discolored, and weakened, and finally kill the plant. They are so small they usually require a magnifying lens to be seen.

40

Araucaria (Norfolk Island pine), 4'

Mealy bugs are easily seen and look similar to small cottony deposits. They tend to be on the undersides of leaves and in the crotches of stems and branches. While they do not spread as rapidly nor do as much damage as spider mites, they can within a few months infect an entire plant, finally weakening and killing it.

Scale is the least common and the least harmful insect. It looks like a small scab and is usually attached to the undersides of leaves and branches. Scale secretes a sticky substance which usually falls to the surface of lower leaves. It has a hard outer shell but is soft and fleshy inside. The dead scale usually do not drop off. If you pick them off and find the shells dry and hollow, they are dead.

There are a few other insects, such as thrip and aphids, but these are far less common indoors than those mentioned above. The same systemic insecticide also will control these insects.

Soil Insects

Soil insects can easily find their way indoors and can also lay dormant in the soil for many months before becoming active. They are harmful to most plants, especially within the restricted soil area of a pot. Occasionally probe the soil to look for moving insects. The plant may even be removed from its pot for an inspection of the roots. If some of the roots are hollow, soil insects (often requiring a magnifying lens to be seen) may be eating the heart of the root, leaving the bark or outer shell behind. Soil insects can cause a plant to turn yellow and even wilt, as they eat the root system which supplies food and water to the plant.

One application of a special soil insecticide is usually sufficient. Preventively, one application every six months is ample protection.

Fungus

Fungus can be either on the foliage or in the soil. Foliar fungus generally shows up as discolored spots on the leaf, or else entire parts of a leaf may look rotten. Soil fungus is also indicated when stems and roots show signs of becoming soft or rotten. It is best to use a systemic fungicide. Like foliage systemic insecticide, it is taken into the plant's system, making it poisonous to most fungus. It is best to spray fungicide on the foliage and then pour the remaining mixture into the soil. As with the control of foliage insects, the best way to ensure that your plants are free from fungus is to treat them with a good fungicide once a month. There is no harm in spraying the fungicide and the insecticide one after the other.

Cleaning the Leaves

It is important to keep foliage clean. Not only are clean plants more attractive, they grow better. Leaves covered with dust are denied the light they need. We suggest

Chlorophytum (spider plant), 1½' *Spathiphyllum,* 1½'

sponging the leaves with a solution of mild soap, well diluted. Any of the varieties of plant cleaning sprays and solutions which impart a shine to the leaf are also good.

Trimming

Most tropical plants and trees continually shed old leaves and grow new ones. In northern climates deciduous plants shed all their leaves once a year in the fall. In temperate or tropical climates this process of losing leaves and growing new ones goes on steadily. Leaves have a life span of a few months to a few years. Unattended outdoors, leaves first turn yellow and finally dry up and drop off. Indoors, we remove the leaves as soon as they turn yellow. They no longer serve any function and detract from the plant's appearance.

Sometimes it is better to trim a leaf rather than remove it. The tips of leaves will often turn brown, particularly on older leaves. Under indoor conditions this happens frequently. Just as yellow leaves should be removed, so should the brown tips be trimmed. It does not harm the leaf to trim the end with scissors to match its natural shape.

Chamaedorea erumpens (bamboo palm), 6′

Pruning

Indoor plants can and should be pruned from time to time. Plants which grow too tall or become thin and leggy can be pruned back. It makes no difference where you cut. Wherever you cut, new shoots will soon develop into foliage and branches. Pruning promotes fullness, as a single pruned trunk or branch can sprout as many as four new stems. Consider how you want the plant to look after it has grown new branches and cut accordingly.

Tolmiea (piggyback), 1½′   *Asparagus,* 1½′

This practice also applies to small new growth on large plants. It is sometimes called "pinching." Removing even a few inches of new growth will result in the branching of two or more new stems from the point of pinching.

The stalk or branch you cut can be put in water or wet potting mix (see p. 48) and in most cases will develop roots. It can then be planted into a pot.

Repotting

As a general rule, indoor plants should be kept in pots as small as possible without overcrowding the root structure. In this way, the activity of the plant growth can be concentrated above ground. Because water and fertilizer are provided and because the plant does not need stability against the wind, an extensive root structure is not required as it would be outdoors. When the roots become a tangled mass pushing against the pot, it is time to give them more space. Long before the plant needs repotting, roots may come out the drainage holes in the bottom of the pot. When you do repot, it is best to use a pot only one or two sizes larger. To repot or inspect the roots, lay the plant on its side and gently tap off the pot. If you go to a larger pot, press the planting mix firmly in the new space around the roots.

Pleomele, 3'

Ficus lyrata (fiddleleaf), 4′

Clay vs. Plastic Pots

Virtually all commercial growers now use plastic or metal pots for growing indoor plants. The main reason is cost, but clay pots have the added disadvantage that diseases can sometimes be harbored in their porous surfaces. However, this disease factor is seldom encountered, and clay pots are more natural-looking and their porosity makes it almost impossible to overwater a plant. If you like the look and don't mind watering often, don't hesitate to use them.

Plastic pots hold the moisture better which saves watering and does not harm the plant if the watering instructions we give are followed.

Soil

Proper indoor planting mix cannot be dug from the back yard. Improper soil becomes hard and unsatisfactory in the small space of a pot. Non-soil planting mixes, such as peat moss, are now in wide use by commercial growers. We have had great success with such mixes ourselves.

Roots grow considerably better in the soft texture of these mixtures such as all peat moss, or a combination of peat moss with vermiculite, of peat moss with perlite, or of all three. These mixes also hold moisture for the roots to gradually absorb and yet allow fast drainage of excess water. They are also lighter in weight.

Be sure to pre-soak the peat moss thoroughly before planting, and pack it into the pot as tightly as possible.

Peat moss, vermiculite, and perlite contain no nutritive value for the plant, so fertilizer must be used. Since you must fertilize a container-grown plant within a few months regardless of how rich the soil, it is obviously better to fertilize from the beginning and put your plant in the planting mix which will be the best medium for your plant's roots over the long run.

If you do choose a regular potting soil, try to get one with at least 50% peat moss.

Going on Trips and Moving

If you're going on a trip and can't arrange for someone to look after your plants, your only problem is watering. For smaller plants, you can either take them to a friend or use various self-watering devices. Larger plants can often go a month between waterings even on a normal basis. *Planting Directly into a Container* on p. 58 gives a method which will self-water plants for up to six months, depending on the size of container. You can also plant a lot of small plants into a large container so they can be self-watered by this method.

Crassula (Chinese jade), 2′

Another technique is putting a plastic bag over the plant to hold moisture. This will double the normal time between waterings. Be sure not to seal the bag completely, and to keep the plant and bag out of direct sunlight which will generate excessive heat inside the bag and damage the plant.

If you're moving, don't be afraid to take your plants along. Just pay careful attention to temperatures—during the move plants should not be subjected to below 40°F. or much above 100°F. Since moving vans don't normally provide such protection, try to use a car. If desirable, you can lay plants on their sides for days at a time provided you protect the foliage and tape crumpled newspaper against the soil to keep it from falling out. If it's very cold, wrap the plants thoroughly because even a few minutes of sub-freezing temperatures can damage them.

Plants can endure being without light at all for up to a week if this proves necessary in the move.

Philodendron pertusum (elephant ears), 2½′

The Psychology of Plants

Much has been written about the possible psychological needs of plants. Research on the subject is being done by institutions such as universities, botanical gardens, and the Department of Agriculture. To date, however, it hasn't been proven that playing music or talking to plants will make them grow better. If it had, obviously this would be an industry-wide practice, but few, if any, commercial growers apply such techniques.

This is not to say it's untrue or impossible. Undoubtedly there is a correlation between the way people feel about their plants and how well the plants survive. Those who care enough for their plants to give them psychological consideration are surely going to take the best possible care of the plants' physical needs, such as watering, and light.

Checking Your Plant's Health

This guide tells all you need to know if you feel your plant is not doing well. The only exception is a plant disease, which would be a rare case. To date, very little research has been done on ornamental plant disease and therefore it is extremely difficult to cure if it appears. Any problem you have is more likely to lie in one of the areas covered by the guide:

• Make sure your plant is getting at least the minimum light rating given in the guide.

• Make sure you are watering properly. Too much water damages roots. With part of the root system destroyed, the plant cannot get enough moisture. This will cause the plant to turn yellow and dry out, the same reaction it has with too little water.

• Check for indications of insects or fungus and treat any such problem accordingly.

• Lack of fertilizer will never cause a dramatic change in a plant's health, but can easily contribute to its gradual deterioration.

• Make sure your plant has not been subjected to any extremes of temperature.

• Too small a pot certainly will not cause rapid deterioration, but will eventually stunt the plant's growth.

51

Kentia, 5′

DECORATIVE PLANT CONTAINERS

Most indoor plants are grown in inexpensive plastic or metal containers which can be decoratively improved in some way, or the plants can be placed into decorative outer containers. Regardless of the approach used, there must be a saucer or other container to collect excess water from the drainage holes which are in the bottom of all *growing* containers.

Terrariums

Plants in terrariums are no different from those in pots. Light requirements are the same and so is watering, although it takes longer between waterings as described in *Watering*, p. 32.

Hanging Baskets

Many of the plants listed on our Survival Chart are suitable for and generally available in hanging baskets. If you acquire plants in standard pots you can repot them into hanging baskets just as you would into other pots or containers. A plant in a hanging basket should be selected and cared for the same as if it were in a regular pot.

Painting Plant Containers

The least expensive approach is to paint the container the plant is growing in. Then place it in a rubber or metal saucer to catch the drainage water.

Clay Pots

Transplanting into a clay pot placed in a clay saucer is the next least expensive improvement. Put a wood spacer or cork disc under the saucer, as drainage water can make a clay saucer damp.

HDP Decorative Containers

Customary ceramic and fiberglas decorative containers are quite expensive. To solve this problem, we developed and now manufacture attractive and inexpensive HDP (high-density polyethlylene) watertight containers. They have straight cylindrical sides, a square inner lip, and a smooth satin finish. The sizes are specifically made to fit the standard containers indoor plants are grown in. As these are the least expensive and most versatile containers available today, they are now being made by a number of manufacturers and are becoming more readily available around the country. Many of the containers in the illustrations in this book are our HDP containers.

Baskets

Baskets make excellent decorative outer containers. A saucer must be placed at the bottom to collect drainage water. Look between the basket and the plant container when watering to make sure some water comes through into the saucer.

Because regular baskets are somewhat costly, we had special basket cylinders woven for us in Haiti. They are not only inexpensive but are very practical. The plant's container is placed on a saucer and the basket cylinder goes over and covers both. It looks exactly like a more expensive basket with a bottom, but has the advantage that you can easily lift the cylinder up to check the amount of water in the saucer after watering. These will probably become commonly available before long, as have the HDP containers.

Podocarpus, 4'

Dracaena warneckei, 2½'

MAKING DECORATIVE PLANTINGS

If you decide to use a decorative outer container, remember that most of them are watertight, without drainage holes. Whether you sit the plant's own container inside one or plant directly into one, it is important to avoid excess drainage water. The installing and planting techniques in this section show how to check drainage water levels easily and how outer containers can act as self-watering devices.

Decorative Outer Containers

If you prefer to just sit the plant's own container inside the decorative one, the plant's container should be raised up a couple inches on pieces of Styrofoam or other material to prevent it from standing in excess drainage water.

Check after each watering to be sure the water has not risen to the bottom of the plant's container. You may look down the gap between the two containers, but it is difficult to tell the depth of the water. A better and more permanent method is to stand a rigid, hollow plastic tube in the gap, extending slightly above the top of the outer container. Take a stick the same height and notch it to show a water level point that is ½″ *below the bottom of the inside container* as it sits on the Styrofoam in the outer one. Leave the stick in the tube, and as with checking the oil level in a car you can "read" the drainage water depth on the stick after each watering.

Remember, if a plant sits in water for more than a couple of days its roots will begin to rot, so any excess water over the notch mark must be removed. The suction hose of a syringe or pump may be put down the plastic tube for easy removal of this excess water. Otherwise,

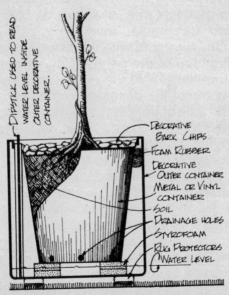

PLANT IN POT INSIDE OUTER DECORATIVE CONTAINER

lift out the plant container and pour away the excess water from the outer container. If you water correctly, you shouldn't have to do this often.

Foam rubber or similar material can be used to cover the small gap at the top between the plant's container and the outside decorative container. This allows placing a decorative covering of moss or bark chips over the entire surface. The rim of the plant's container is then hidden, making it look as if the plant has been planted directly into the decorative container.

Planting Directly into a Decorative Container

Planting directly into a watertight decorative container is quite practical and has the advantage of allowing long periods between waterings, especially with larger containers. The planting procedure is simple. Start with horticultural-grade perlite at the bottom of the container. Construction-grade perlite, available at building-supply stores, is also acceptable. Then remove the plant from its growing container and without disturbing the roots or soil, place it on top of the perlite. Make the perlite deep enough so that the top of the plant's soil level is about ½″ below the top of the decorative container. Place perlite around the side of the plant as well, using soil only on the top inch for appearance. The perlite acts like a sponge, carrying any excess drainage water at the bottom of the container back up to the plant.

Gravel at the bottom of a container is worthless. The drainage water will simply sit in the bed of gravel and stagnate, as gravel does not have the ability to carry the excess drainage water back up to the plant's root system. Perlite, on the other hand, will easily carry water as much as 12″ upward. The porous, granular perlite also allows water to be stored at the bottom of the container. The plant draws water as it needs it. This allows you to leave the plant unattended for months at a time.

Care must be taken not to put too much water in the container, as standing water will damage the plant's roots. Standing water should never rise higher than a level just below the plant's roots at the time it was planted (1″ below if you have room). To identify this point we use a technique similar to that given in *Decorative Outer Containers*, p. 56. At the time of planting, place a

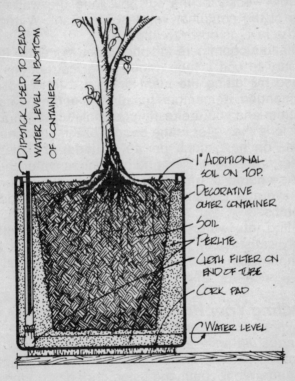

DIPSTICK USED TO READ WATER LEVEL IN BOTTOM OF CONTAINER.

1″ ADDITIONAL SOIL ON TOP.

DECORATIVE OUTER CONTAINER

SOIL

PERLITE

CLOTH FILTER ON END OF TUBE

CORK PAD

WATER LEVEL

PLANTING DIRECTLY INTO DECORATIVE CONTAINER

rigid plastic tube in the container to extend from the bottom of the container to above the soil on top. Take a stick the same height and notch it to indicate the maximum acceptable water level. Put the stick inside the tube and you can then use it to read the depth of the drainage water. Cover the bottom of the tube with a filter to prevent any perlite from getting into the tube. At first, check every few weeks to find out how long the water in the bottom of the container will last the plant. Water again when the level is down to about ¼".

In shallow containers (4" and under in depth) it is not necessary to use a tube. Modify the instructions under *Watering* by letting the plant dry out a little more than recommended. Remember, the plant is getting water from the bottom and you are testing for moisture from the top.

How long the water in the bottom of the container lasts depends on how much perlite is under the plant, the diameter of the container, and how much water the plant uses. As a guide, 3" of water in an 18" diameter container under average conditions will last a plant as long as six months.

Planting into watertight containers by this method is not only satisfactory for plants, it also provides a self-watering system which is reliable for plants of all sizes.

Protecting Your Rugs and Floors

Drainage water in a waterproof container can sometimes cause external condensation which can damage a rug or floor. We recommend using cork or wooden bases to eliminate this possibility.

The large bottom of a heavy container can permanently flatten the nap of a rug. We recommend using a number of spiked plastic feet under the container to protect the nap.

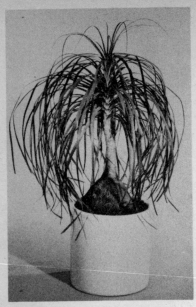

Beaucarnea (pony tail), 3½′

Hoya (wax plant), 2′

WHERE YOUR PLANTS COME FROM

As commercial growers and retailers, we've found that many people want to know where their plants come from. A few words about our nurseries will give you an idea. Indoor plants are tropical plants and the only economical place to grow them is in the tropics. Florida is where most are grown, and where we have our largest nursery, near the southern tip of the state. Here we propagate most of our own plants, often using an extensive misting system.

We also acquire plants from among 6000 other tropical-plant nurseries spread throughout southern Florida, most of which are very small. Our trucks and buyers cover considerable distances to bring high-quality plants back to our nursery, where we sometimes grow them further, and always condition them for the northern indoor environment.

We do this by maintaining the plants under deep shade until they have become completely adjusted to indoor light conditions. This is accomplished in shade houses which have a covering of a heavy mesh plastic screening, so heavy that only 13% of the Florida sunlight gets through to the plants underneath.

Although Florida is the most convenient place to grow plants for the United States market, they grow much faster in warmer tropical climates. Puerto Rico's average winter temperature is only 5°F. below the summer average, and as the island has high humidity, it's an ideal growing climate for us. Everything from our nursery there is shipped by air to the one in Florida to be conditioned for shipment north.

For that, we have long-distance tractor-trailers which are temperature-controlled to maintain a constant 60°F. We pack the plants tightly against each other, the big ones on the floor and the small ones on shelves. Most of the time, we are able to ship our plants unboxed, so that air may freely circulate around them. Experience has taught us that this is the best way to ensure that the plants are in the hardiest possible condition when they get to the consumer.

Euphorbia (candelabra plant), 2′

Nephthytis, 1½'

Filices (fern), 1½'

A LAST WORD

Many people from out of town ask us if they can get plants or accessories by mail. Unfortunately, shipping plants by mail, particularly large plants, is not practical as in most cases the lack of temperature control during transit will cause damage. Only if the order were large enough for us to ship direct from our Florida nursery could we be sure of temperature control, because we would be using our own trucks. It will probably be easier for you to buy your plants locally and use our advice on how to select and care for them.

We can, however, supply the following accessories if you are unable to find them locally: Haitian basket cylinders from 6″ to 22″ diameter, black or white HDP (high-density polyethylene) decorative containers in 10″ to 22″ diameter, and slow-release fertilizers in both basic-element and trace-element formulas. Please write to us in New York and we will mail you a price sheet. Our address is 409 E. 60th Street, N.Y., N.Y. 10022, telephone 212-PLaza 8-8181.

We hope you have found this book sufficiently direct and concise to enable you to quickly and easily understand the fundamentals of selecting and caring for your plants. There are few investments which will give you as much pleasure for your money as a growing indoor plant.

—Terrestris

INDEX